ART MUSEUMS IN AMERICA.

(*FROM "OLD AND NEW" FOR APRIL*, 1870.)

BY

GEORGE F. COMFORT.

BOSTON:
H. O. HOUGHTON AND COMPANY,
135 WASHINGTON STREET.
1870.

ART MUSEUMS IN AMERICA.

In the great intellectual awakening, which has followed our late national convulsion, the public attention has been turned in a marked degree to certain deficiencies in our educational system. Especially has the lack been felt of those institutions for the promotion of æsthetic culture, which are found in every nation and almost in every city in Europe. That this feeling is a deep conviction, and not a superficial, evanescent flush of sentiment, is shown by the tangible form which it has assumed in some of our largest cities. Movements for establishing extensive museums of the fine-arts were inaugurated in the cities of New York and Boston at almost the same time. These two movements, though begun under very different circumstances, still look to the same ultimate end. Without doubt other cities will soon follow the example of Boston and New York.

The fine-arts are divided into two classes: those which appeal to the soul through the channel of the ear, termed in German the "speaking" (redende) arts, the chief representatives of which are oratory, poetry, and music; and those which appeal to the soul through the channel of the eye, termed in English the formative arts, the chief representatives of which are architecture, sculpture, and painting.

By a peculiar combination of circumstances, the first of the "speaking" arts, oratory, has been developed in America to a degree of perfection far surpassing that attained by any other art, and equalling or surpassing that attained by this art in any other country. In the second of the speaking arts, poetry, America is fully equal to any other land; we have several poets, as Longfellow, Bryant, and Lowell, who are not surpassed by the contemporary poets of any other nation. In the third of the speaking arts, music, America is far behind every country in Europe. We have scarcely an eminent American composer, and our conservatories of music are only in the bud.

But in the formative arts, in architecture, sculpture, painting, and in the application of art to industry, America is markedly in the back-ground. With us, the usual order of history has been reversed. Thus in Egypt, in Greece and her colonies, in Italy and other mediæval countries of Europe, the fine arts (using the term now in its restricted sense, as applying to the formative arts) flourished with great luxuriance in the early periods of national development. But here in America, after two hundred and fifty years of national growth, we have scarcely begun to cultivate the formative arts, upon a scale at all commensurate with the immediate wants of the country, and with the culture of the present age.

Still in no country in the world is there more native genius for art than in America. There has always been a "faithful few" among architects, who have struggled against the control which mere "builders" have acquired over their art. This control is now nearly broken, even in the rural districts. The rapid progress which has been made in both ecclesiastical and civil architecture during the last ten years, is an index of the high state which that art will soon attain among us. We have also a few sculptors who deserve honorable mention among the best representatives of the plastic art in the world; and in painting an Allston, a Stuart, and a Cole, and others in past generations, have been worthy predecessors of the very respectable number of artists who, in two or three of our cities, have brought at least landscape and portrait painting, to a degree of excellence, rivalling that attained in any other country. If art has arrived at its present condition in a few even of our cities under such discouraging circumstances, with no schools for instruction, with a general indifference on the part of the general public, and with but a spasmodic and sporadic patronage, what excellence might it not have attained, had there been as high regard for its influence, and as much time, attention, and money devoted to instruction in it, as have been given to natural science, to mathematics, Latin, or Greek, and had art been patronized by the whole of the people in every part of the land. A few of our men of wealth have collected, at great expense, very excellent private galleries of art. But the general fact remains that we are without academies of art, and that the public have little knowledge of the principles of true taste.

By our neglect of the fine-arts we are contradicting, in a most singular manner, our claims and reputation as a practical people. More buildings are erected annually in America, than in half, if not than in the whole of Europe. And yet we have not a single academy of architecture, or school of the fine-arts in general. Little Belgium, on the other hand, with a population about equal to that of the State of New York, with one fourth its territory, and perhaps one half its material wealth, has three academies of the fine-arts in general (at Brussels, Antwerp, and Bruges), and sixty-five schools of design, which are attended by over twelve thousand pupils. In a liberal system of education, this branch should receive as much time and attention as chemistry, algebra, Latin, Greek, or French. But formal instruction in the principles and the practice of art, is not sufficient. It is as necessary for the young artist to see the exemplification of the principles of art in the works of the great masters, as it is for the medical student to witness the operations of skillful physicians and surgeons in the clinique; and to the public, a good painting, statue, or cathedral is a more forcible and effective educator in the principles of true taste, than a long series of lessons or lectures. Hence the necessity for art-museums.

An edifice which is to contain public galleries of art, should be located away from the noisy and dusty thoroughfares of a great city; it should be placed where no other buildings will ever be erected in its immediate vicinity, which, by their shadows and reflections of light may make the rooms unserviceable as galleries of art; it should be placed where there will be opportunity for such indefinite expansion as may be required by the wants of the future; and it should be within easy access of the great mass of the population of the city. All of these conditions can be met with only in the public parks. In the chief park of every city, a plot should be left, upon which museum buildings of both science and art may be placed. This plot should be near the edge of the park, and in the vicinity of other institutions for the higher education, as schools of art and of practical science, colleges, universities, and public libraries, — all of which should be located within a convenient distance of each other. In this respect the city of Berlin has a great advantage over any other city in the world, and by this means the efficiency of all its institutions is greatly increased.

By their own example, the museum buildings should be promoters of one of the chief arts which their contents illustrate. They should be landmarks in the history of architecture in America. So great is now the *solidarité*, the coherence and intercourse between nations, that any new excellence which may be developed in one land is soon known, and is likely to be reproduced in other lands. We might therefore with as much propriety speak of American chemistry, astronomy, medicine, or music, as of American architecture. The museum buildings should, therefore, be landmarks, — not of American architecture, but of architecture in America, and they should mark a progress in the history of architecture in the world. And in its interior arrangement, a museum building should be planned with special reference to the purpose which the edifice is to serve.

In considering the contents of museums of art in America, we will first speak of those which may be established in our largest cities, — as New York, Boston, Philadelphia, Baltimore, Cincinnati, Chicago, St. Louis, and San Francisco. We will then speak of what it is possible to accomplish in cities of less size and wealth. We will also make a few suggestions with reference to the establishment of museums in smaller places. For very much may be accomplished even in our smaller towns. Indeed, the superiority of Europe over America in institutions of high culture, is seen in no phase in a more striking light than by comparing the small cities with each other. Thus the city of Gotha is about as large as Newburg, having about seventeen thousand inhabitants. The entire Duchy of Saxe-Coburg-Gotha is almost identical in size with Orange County, N. Y.; the material wealth of the two is not very different. But Gotha has a museum of art, containing over seven hundred excellent paintings, fifty thousand engravings, forty thousand coins (with casts of fourteen thousand more), nine thousand drawings, a large collection of casts of works of sculpture and architecture, and many other works of art; the city also contains a fine museum of natural history, an observatory, a gymnasium (or college), a polytechnic school, a school of trade and business, and a library of a hundred and sixty thousand volumes, with many miniatures and manuscripts; — (the library was founded the same year as Harvard College, in 1640, and all the other institutions are of modern origin).

A museum of art in a large and wealthy city should illustrate the history of the origin, the rise, the growth, the culminating glory, and the periods of decline and decadence of all the formative arts, both pure and applied, as they have appeared in all lands and in all ages of the world. True art is cosmopolitan. It knows no country; it knows no age. Homer sang, not for the Greeks alone, but for all nations and for all time. Beethoven is the musician, not of the Germans alone, but of all cultivated nations. And Raphael painted, not for the Italians alone, but for all, of whatever land or age, whose hearts are open to sympathy with the beautiful in art. An ideal museum must thus be cosmopolitan in its character; and it must present the whole stream of art-history in all nations and ages, as represented in the three great arts, of architecture, sculpture, and painting, in the minor arts, and in the many applications of art to industry, by the adornment of every material production which comes from the hand of man.

A work of art thus studied historically has other charms, besides its own intrinsic merits, as of beauty of composition, color, form, execution, or expression. It serves as a link in the great æsthetic development of the human race, and thus aids us to see the unity of the history of art, from the building of the first pyramids down to the present time. The history of art thus studied becomes an integral part of the history of civilization. And a collateral, but a by no means unimportant advantage to be derived from the study of art historically, is the interest which it awakens and the light that it throws upon the great events and the prominent characters in universal history; upon the customs, costumes, and daily life of different peoples and in different ages; and upon the moral, religious, intellectual, industrial, and political progress of the human race.

To establish a museum covering thus the entire history of art is a vast undertaking. At a first glance it may seem impossible. We will proceed to consider how far it is feasible.

With reference to sculpture success is more easily attained than in any other branch of the fine arts. It is indeed possible to reproduce every existing work of sculpture in the world. During the latter part of the last century Raphael Mengs founded the Museum of Sculpture in Dresden, by gathering casts in plaster of Paris of the chief works of classic art, which were then known. The value of this museum is now increased by the fact that some of the originals have since been destroyed, and that those works are now to be studied only through these casts. Since the death of Raphael Mengs the collection has been greatly enlarged by the addition of casts of representative works of all periods. The New Museum in Berlin offers, through its magnificent collection of casts, better opportunities for studying the history of plastic art than are to be found in any other single museum in the world. The museum building was completed in 1855, and the whole of this unrivalled collection of casts has been procured within a few years. This method of reproducing works of sculpture, by means of plaster casts, has been adopted extensively in many public and private museums in Europe. One Prussian nobleman has a gallery of casts at his country seat, upon which he has expended over a hundred thousand thalers. There are large collections in the University of Bonn, in the city of Gotha, in the Louvre, and in the Kensington Museum (one of the most interesting and useful museums in the world), and in other museums in France, Germany, and Italy. All of the works of Thorwaldsen are represented, mostly by casts, in a building erected to contain them, in Copenhagen; a building in Munich contains a complete collection of casts of the work of the great Bavarian sculptor, Schwanthaler; there is a similar collection of casts of the works of Rauch in Berlin; and of Tieck in Dresden. In a great museum, separate rooms could be set apart to contain casts of many or all the works of the most important sculptors.

Casts in plaster of Paris have many advantages over copies in marble. They are perfectly accurate reproductions of the originals. The texture of the surface is soft and mellow, in some qualities surpassing even marble. For purposes of study and for real æsthetic effect they are better than most original antiques, as they are entirely free from discolorations occasioned by exposure for fifteen or twenty centuries to the action of the weather, or to the dampness of the soil in which they have lain imbedded. The color and general appearance of works in bronze can be perfectly reproduced by bronzing the surface of the casts; as they are strengthened by an iron frame on the inside, they may be used to represent very light and slender works in bronze.

Many persons, of much culture even, have been led by the fact that the country is flooded with peddlers, who vend for trifling sums poor casts of inferior works, to consider all casts to be unartistic, vulgar, and unworthy of a place in the gallery of a gentleman of taste, or in a museum of art. But they overlook the fact that the genius of a sculptor is shown in the composition, the movement, the accuracy and delicacy of form, and the expression of his works; that it does not lie in the material he employs, be it marble, bronze, terra-cotta, wood, or plaster, and that a perfect copy is as good as an original, for all purposes of study, and for æsthetic effect. The cheapness of casts will be a stumbling-block to many dilettanti and snobs, but it will be a recommendation with men of sense and with all true lovers of art for the sake of art. The question of the propriety of introducing casts into museums of art has been practically settled, by the great and increasing popularity of the magnificent collection in the museum at Berlin, the most cultivated city in the world. A more extensive collection than that in Berlin even, is contemplated in Paris. The trustees of the museum in Boston have wisely determined to begin, by making an extensive collection of casts of antique sculpture.

There are some disadvantages, however, with plaster casts. Though the interior iron frame makes them very strong, the surface is much more fragile than marble. Great care is also necessary to avoid exposure to dust; not even the lightest feather should touch the surface of those that are not bronzed, but dust should be blown off by bellows; the floors of the rooms containing them should never be swept, but they should be cleansed by means of a wet cloth, as is done in the museums of painting and sculpture in Europe. A strange fascination, also, attaches to the identical stone or bronze of an antique, even though it be an ancient copy of another original, or though this antique be so discolored that its true artistic effect can only be discerned through means of a plaster cast. It is, of course, highly important that the cast be not made in a careless manner, nor from an imperfect mould.

It would be well for the Boston and New York museums to unite in procuring new moulds, instead of importing separate collections of casts. The little additional expense thus incurred would soon be made up by the sale of casts to other museums, which will soon be organized in our other chief cities. The British Museum, and the museums of Berlin, Munich, and the Louvre, among others, greatly increase their efficiency as promoters of æsthetic culture by disposing of casts from originals or moulds which are in their possession. A commission from all the chief museums in Europe, is now arranging for having moulds taken of all the important works in their possession. May we not hope that the first complete collection of casts thus formed may be made in some American city!

Prominent works of sculpture, of which it is not convenient, or of which it is not permitted to take casts, can be represented with excellent effect by engravings or photographs.

Though most of the important original works of ancient and mediæval, and nearly all the works of modern sculpture are either *in loco* and never will be moved, or are already transferred permanently to the great museums of Europe, still many originals of much value are brought to the market from time to time by the sale of private collections. With every year the supply from this source is rapidly diminishing. Turkey is the only remaining country in which original antiques are found, where the government has not forbidden their exportation. The director of the classical department of the museum of Berlin is at this very time in the island of Cyprus, for the purpose of examining a collection of Grecian antiquities and works of art, which the American Consul in that island has been gathering during the last few years, with reference to purchasing them for the Berlin Museum. But a word only from the Sultan is necessary, such as was given by the Viceroy of Egypt a short time ago, to close up this last remaining source of undiscovered works of Greek art. If we expect ever to have any valuable original antiques, we must move quickly.

In the illustration of architecture we meet with more difficulties. It is of course impossible to reproduce in full size the great temples of antiquity, or the cathedrals of the Middle Ages. Yet a very good impression of the style and general effect of works of architecture can be given by means of models in cork, alabaster, and other materials. What has been said of reproducing works of sculpture by casts, applies equally well to reproducing the ornamentation, the characteristic feature, of the different styles of architecture. The Berlin, the Kensington, and other museums of Europe contain large collections of casts of capitals and bases of columns, sections of columns, mouldings, corbels, and other ornamentation from works in the different periods of architecture. Many of the larger architectural features also, as pulpits, pinnacles, pendants, windows, and entire doorways, with their rich ornamentation and their sculpture, can be reproduced in full size by means of casts. All who have been in the Sydenham Palace will remember the remarkable interest awakened by the restoration of some entire rooms, as from Egyptian and Grecian temples, from houses in Pompeii, and from the Alhambra. While the details are thus given in full size, the effect of the whole edifice can be given by models in cork, or by photographs, engravings, and drawings, which can be taken from different positions, so as to present the various parts of the exterior and the interior.

The time is past when we could procure for our museums many important paintings by the old masters. Nearly all of their chief works, which are not permanently attached to the walls where they were painted or placed, are already gathered into the great museums of Europe. There are, however, many paintings by the old masters, of greater or less merit, in the possession of private persons, which from time to time are offered for sale. Thus, some very excellent originals by Titian, Tintoretto, Andrea del Sarto, Memling, Rubens, Paul Potter, Teniers, and other great mediæval painters, will be disposed of this spring at the sale in Paris of the great Demidoff gallery, one of the finest collections of works of art ever gathered by a private person. But the opportunities for purchasing such originals are rapidly passing away; and while the supply is diminishing, the demand is increasing; only by being upon the alert immediately, therefore, can we procure any important work by the old masters.

These comparatively inferior originals will serve an important purpose in museums, as giving examples of the artist's own work, of the touch of his own pencil, even if they be not of his happiest moods. But, on the other hand, they may do great injury. Those artists and others, who are not familiar with the masterpieces of the old painters, will receive very inadequate and false impressions of their genius and of the glory of their great works, by seeing only these their inferior productions. But this evil may be remedied to a certain extent. The composition, the drawing, the light and shade of all the great paintings, may be reproduced perfectly by means of photographs and engravings. In no other way has the art of photography done more for the promotion of æsthetic culture, than by the facility it has given to the dissemination of a knowledge of the history of painting.

Some of the greatest works in the entire history of art, as Leonardo's "Last Supper," are known to us only through means of copies. In many of the galleries of the most cultivated English noblemen, and of other connoisseurs and patrons of art, are to be found most excellent copies of the masterpieces of the great painters. By commissioning only mature and first-class artists, who are in sympathy with the spirit of the old masters, we can form a gallery, which will present a better view of the rise and progress of painting and of the many schools of this branch of art, than is to be had in any single gallery now existing in the world. Many first-class artists would doubtless feel it a sacrifice to devote even a year, to copying the works of their predecessors. But, besides being remunerated as well as though producing original works, they would find a reward in the fact that they were assisting to found a museum in which the history of this art in its entirety could be seen and studied for generations and centuries to come. It is due also to art and to civilization, that copies, equalling the originals as nearly as possible, should be made of every masterpiece of painting. Some of the best paintings are crumbling under the hand of time. Many are in buildings that are not fire-proof. By an unfortunate fire in the vestry of the Church of Sts. John and Paul, about two years ago, more than a dozen valuable paintings by Titian, Bellini, and others were burnt up. And it is easy to foresee circumstances under which whole galleries of art may be destroyed.

Drawings and sketches by the old masters form a very interesting feature in the museums of Europe. These drawings are perfectly reproduced by photography. Thus, by means of this art, we can make collections which will contain perfect copies of all the valuable drawings in the different museums in the world.

The illumination of manuscripts,—formerly termed miniature painting,—is a most interesting branch of art, which existed from the sixth to the fifteenth century, but which went into disuse on the invention of printing. Occasionally an excellent original miniature painting can yet be procured. But generally new museums will have to depend upon reproductions by chromolithography or upon copies made by hand. Besides being beautiful as works of art in themselves, illuminations are valuable for the light which they throw upon the history of the other branches of painting.

The history of the rise and progress of engraving, in all its branches, from the invention of printing down to the present time, should be fully illustrated in a great museum. The old Pinakothek, in Munich, contains over three hundred thousand engravings; the museum in Berlin, over five hundred thousand; and the Imperial Library in Paris, over a million and a quarter. Not only do these collections illustrate the history of engraving as a separate art, but the engravings themselves, like the illuminations which they displaced, throw much light upon the history of the other arts, and also upon the general history of civilization.

A great deal of artistic skill has been applied in different ages to the ornamentation of medallions, precious stones, jewelry, porcelain wares and other articles, whose only use is the adornment of the person or of the apartments of dwelling-houses. Especially has taste been displayed in the ornamentation of coins. Medallions and coins can be reproduced by copies in plaster, as is done so extensively in the museum of Gotha. These casts can be gilded, so as to represent the originals perfectly. It would be easy thus to form, at a moderate expense, a collection of casts of the best coins and medallions in the different museums, which would greatly excel in artistic value, and for the purposes of study, the most extensive and costly collection of originals in the world. The Greeks paid especially great attention to the ornamentation of vases, and the Etruscans to the ornamentation of metallic mirrors, with scenes from their history and mythologies. Vases can be reproduced in terra-cotta, and galvano-plastic copies can be taken of the metallic mirrors. All of these minor arts, also, are valuable for the light which they throw not only upon the æsthetic culture, but upon the mythology, the history, and the general civilization of the countries, and the ages, in which they have existed.

Another important purpose to be served by a great museum, is the illustration of the history of the application of art to industry, as shown in the ornamentation of furniture of all kinds, as chairs, tables, chests, candelabras, chandeliers, the locks and hinges of doors, tapestry for the floor and for walls; of chalices and other utensils for church service; of armor and the instruments of warfare; of religious and civil garments and costumes; and in short in the ornamentation of every material production or instrument which is made by the hand of man. Indeed, during every great period of artistic development and æsthetic culture, the purer and the applied arts have gone hand in hand, and have supplemented and mutually inspired each other. It would be as possible to divorce science, as to divorce art from its application to industry. And it would be contrary to all analogies of history that we should have good architecture, sculpture, and painting in America, without the æsthetic culture produced by the presence of these works manifesting itself in the tasteful ornamentation of our furniture, carpets, household utensils, dress; of the fences around our houses; of carriages, railroad cars, machinery, tools; and in short of every material object and instrument which we employ, and by which we are surrounded. And in return, the tasteful ornamentation of the objects and utensils of daily life, will insensibly develop an æsthetic culture which will be offended by poor works in the high arts of architecture, sculpture, and painting. Many beautiful articles of ancient, especially of Egyptian, and of mediæval furniture, of majolica ware, armor, and domestic and ecclesiastical utensils, can yet be procured. The more choice ones have, however, already been gathered into the great museums of Europe. But they can be represented by engravings, photographs, and in some cases by copies in plaster and papier maché.

Great museums of art should look to the future also, as well as to the past; and every great museum building should have a wing capable of indefinite extension, for the reception of such works as may be produced in the future by American artists especially, which shall merit a position beside the works of the old masters. The spaces on the walls of the vestibules, the halls, and the rooms of the museum buildings, will offer opportunities for the display of the highest genius of our own painters. Valuable lessons may be learned in this respect from the successes and the failures in the Glyptothek and Pinakothek in Munich, and in the museum in Berlin. The direct and indirect influence of these museums upon every branch of native art will be most salutary, inspiriting, and almost instantaneous.

Reverting now to the plan of the museum buildings, we repeat that the interior should be designed in its general plan, and in all its details, with special reference to the particular works of art which are to be placed in each individual room and in each suite of rooms. To the degree in which this plan is neglected will the design be a failure. The mistakes which were made twenty and fifty years ago, when museum architecture was in its infancy, were excusable and perhaps unavoidable; but the future will deal severely with our memories, if we impose upon them repetitions of mistakes, which with a little care and foresight we may easily avoid.

The cost of museums which shall thus represent the entire history of past art, and which shall keep progress with the advancement of art in all countries, will be very great, and may be increased to an indefinite extent. But if they are organized upon a reasonable scale, the cost will not be disproportionate to the present and prospective wealth of our chief cities, a few of which are already many times larger and richer than some of the cities in Europe, like Munich, Stuttgart, Carlsruhe, and Berlin, which have established and built up, almost entirely within the last fifty years, their museums and schools of art and science, libraries, universities, and a whole phalanx of institutions of high culture which have no representatives in any city in America. The cost of such a museum would not be greater than it is to build, equip, and sustain a single man-of-war, or twenty miles of an ordinary railroad (and we have nearly forty thousand miles of railway in America); it would not be greater than that of many of the cathedrals which are now being built; nor would it be one fourth of what we are now expending upon our parks. But the organization of such a museum will necessarily be a slow work; it will require at least a generation for its completion; and thus the burden for any single year or term of years will not be unduly severe.

Museums organized upon such a complete, and — as it will seem to us, until we shall have grown to the European conception of such institutions — upon such an immense scale, will be feasible only in our very largest cities, as New York, Boston, Philadelphia, Chicago, and San Francisco. But cities of a lesser size, as Portland, Hartford, Buffalo, Pittsburg, and Cleveland — much larger and richer cities than Carlsruhe, Stuttgart, Antwerp, Ghent, Parma, Modena, or Athens, — can establish museums upon essentially the same plan, but upon a scale proportioned to their relative wealth. A valuable influence can be exercised also upon the public taste and the promotion of good art in America, if the smaller cities, as Bangor, New Haven, Binghampton, and Indianapolis, and even the village of a few thousand inhabitants, as Augusta, Concord, Fall River, New Britain, Waterbury, Ithaca, and Ann Arbor, should establish upon a scale that will not involve an undue expenditure, small museums containing plaster casts, models, engravings, and photographs of works of architecture, sculpture, and painting, and of illustrations of the application of art to industry. A few thousand dollars, wisely spent, would form a museum which would be the means of great enjoyment, culture, and practical value to the inhabitants of a village, and of its adjacent region. Indeed, a single thousand dollars, judiciously expended, would be sufficient to fill a single room with a collection of casts, photographs, and engravings, which might be the nucleus of an excellent village gallery of art, and thus be the promoter of æsthetic culture in an entire community. An energetic committee of gentlemen or ladies could raise that amount within less than a week, in almost any village of five thousand inhabitants. Indeed, it is not by any means certain that finer galleries of art will not be established, at first, in some of the smaller cities, than in those of the largest size.

The temporary success at least of movements to organize museums in our chief cities will depend upon the measures that may be adopted at the outset. Thus, it would be very unwise to expend large sums of money at first upon such a vast edifice as will finally be required for a great gallery of art. The first moneys that may be raised should be devoted to the purchase of works of art. Should no valuable originals be immediately available, the first fifty or hundred thousand dollars should be devoted to commencing a collection of casts, models, engravings, and photographs of the chief representative historic works of architecture, sculpture, and painting. While these are being collected, designs could be made for a tasteful structure of iron and glass, which enterprising builders in any of our chief cities would erect upon a two months' notice. This temporary receptacle of the works of art should be in the vicinity, but not upon the site, of the permanent museum building. It will always be serviceable for the temporary reception of new works, and for loan and other exhibitions, after the permanent edifice is completed.

Even before these museums become fully established, they can accomplish much good by means of loan exhibitions. In every large city, and often in small towns, there are already many valuable works of art, which their possessors would feel an honorable pride in exhibiting to the public for short periods. And even after the museums become so large that no private gallery can compete with them, much interest may be occasionally awakened by these loan exhibitions, which might be held in the edifice erected for the temporary reception of new works of art for the museum. Such loan exhibitions have frequently been held in different cities of Europe, as Prague, Nuremberg, in the Kensington Museum of London, and in many cities of England. Not unfrequently valuable works of art will be loaned for long periods; upon the death of their owners, these will frequently be bequeathed to the museums; it is by this means that the German museum at Nuremberg and the Kensington Museum have received many of their most important works of art. Entire private galleries will also often be bequeathed to these public museums. But great firmness should be shown from the first in not accepting anything merely because it is a gift.

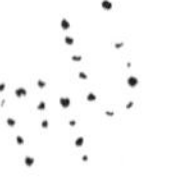

Many important results will be accomplished by these museums. A purer taste will be cultivated throughout the entire community, and art in all its branches will be stimulated into a healthier and more vigorous life; chaste and tasteful ornamentation will replace the glaring colors, gaudy decorations, and bad designs that so often disfigure the furniture and the walls of our dwellings; paintings that offend a cultivated taste will disappear from the walls of our parlors; our streets will be filled with a purer architecture, and our parks with statuary of nobler motive and better execution. It will become fashionable also to visit the museums, as it now is to drive in the park, and to become acquainted with every important new work of art that is received; under the influence of this fashion, a certain portion of the vast sums of money, which are now spent upon luxurious living, expensive furniture, costly clothing, and fast horses, will be devoted to adorning the walls of our own houses with works of high art. That large part of the population, which must be forever prevented from purchasing works of art for their own homes. the poor, will have free access to galleries which no private citizen, whatever his wealth, would ever be able to gather together. And who can tell in how many young minds the germs of genius will be thus developed, which will give a glory to our country and to humanity, but which otherwise would remain dormant and thus be lost to the world!

www.ingramcontent.com/pod-product-compliance
Lightning Source LLC
LaVergne TN
LVHW020638110826
845149LV00004B/1276

* 9 7 8 1 4 1 8 1 8 9 5 1 8 *